CW00764735

KIDLAND
and other poems
PAUL KINGSNORTH

salmonpoetry

Published in 2011 by
Salmon Poetry
Cliffs of Moher, County Clare, Ireland
Website: www.salmonpoetry.com
Email: info@salmonpoetry.com

Copyright © Paul Kingsnorth, 2011

ISBN 978-1-907056-67-3

All rights reserved. No part of this publication may be reproduced or transmitted in any form or by any means, electronic or mechanical, including photography, recording, or any information storage or retrieval system, without permission in writing from the publisher. The book is sold subject to the condition that it shall not, by way of trade or otherwise, be lent, resold or otherwise circulated without the publisher's prior consent in any form of binding or cover other than that in which it is published and without a similar condition, including this condition, being imposed on the subsequent purchaser.

COVER IMAGE: *Forest abstract* © *Glenn Nagel* | *Dreamstime.com*
COVER DESIGN: *Siobhán Hutson*

For Leela and Jeevan, who will come through

Acknowledgements

Acknowledgements are due to the editors of the following publications, in which versions of these poems have previously appeared:

The Lighthouse, Weyfarers, nthposition, The Gibson Poetry Competition (Thomas Hardy Society), and *Re:versing the damage.*

I would also like to thank: Jessie Lendennie, for getting it from the start; Siobhán Hutson for making this collection live on the page; Mario Petrucci, Glyn Hughes and David Knowles for their time and hard-won wisdom; Will Ross for crafting my online presence; the people of the Dark Mountain for scaling the slopes with me; and my family, especially Jyoti, for simply being there.

For man's half dream; man, you might say, is nature dreaming, but rock
And water and sky are constant – to feel
Greatly, and understand greatly, and express greatly, the natural
Beauty, is the sole business of poetry.
The rest's diversion: those holy or noble sentiments, the intricate ideas,
The love, lust, longing: reasons, but not the reason.

ROBINSON JEFFERS, *The Beauty of Things*

Contents

The tower

These are my words: they are the framing timbers
for ideas. It is ideas which destroy worlds.
See, I have pared the rough edges from an experience
and placed its tapestry, its copperplate,
its half convincing fiction before you.
It is a beautiful thing: dig, you may find
some Truth in it. But the shape
is unnatural, it is words only, and the world's greatness
will not fit within them however well
they are shaped. All that will fit is
ideas, stacking pleasingly upon each other until
they make a great tower whose shadow is the shape
of a mass grave, a burning forest, the death
of the seas. The day will come again when we will set it
aflame and dance howling around it,
released from words for a short time,
but long enough.

Prophecy

To the dark gods of the storm clouds, we say:
we are here we are waiting for you

On the snowplaned sides of the unfarmed hills, we say:
approach we are not so civilised yet

Among the red dunes, by the gun grey sea, we say:
we do not want to go back but we know that we will

By the moss drenched riverside, in the ravine, we say:
we play games of escape but we have not escaped

In the yellow streets, hiding from the moon, we say:
we harvest our stories we reap them we bind them

On the tower, watching, they reply:
You have long forked your lightning in the heart of this green.
Now, come home

A haunting

What is this: it has tusks
yet moves softly through the grasses?
What are these: jewelled
and gone now; these, winged
and free in the uncounted trees?
I am alone in this city of mutants
yet there are sounds all around me.
A column of great mammals passes close
then sieves through sodium lighting into blackness,
empty like the sea. Once there were giants
in the Earth. Now the once free
are Useful or gone. I turn,
a shadow passes me, a breath
in the air, the movement of pads
on dark mud. The city grows.
A shadow only now, a shadow
only. In silence, the ape
declares victory.

Then we will go to Europe

Then we will go to Europe, go
to Venice or Berlin, and live like Rilke
in communes of verse and there,
maybe there, we will shake off this disease

which dulls our senses and dulls everything
and spreads like aluminium
and clings like a plastic bag in a high branch,
like crude to a gannet's feathers. Or

if not in the cities then in the forests
or in red caves in red deserts
or around the craters of gunungs in the archipelago
or among sandstone towers in the valleys of the West.
Oh –

I don't know. Just take me
somewhere it has not yet reached, somewhere
lonely and still real and let me
stand there and feel nothing
and lose the fear and, finally,
breathe.

Atlantic low

never to come by here again. And I do not know
what it is all about and I do not care
what it is all about, only that the sun comes
and touches me sometimes and touches the stone
and reminds me. There are trees
on the southern slope, their needles shift in the cloud, shift
under the mountain. Always there is cloud
on the mountain. I dream of the sun,
the sun which touches me when the river speaks,
sun which soaks the stone white, dissolves
the cloud, dissolves the mountain,
dissolves me in it. To be dissolved.

Lights in the desert

Beatty, Nevada

It is a dozen miles to the bald mountain
where, in green, something burns.
More, maybe, to the dead valleys in the east.
In white, there, something was born.

In the skies you feel it; in the wind,
were there any, and in the lying clarity
of a winter darkness it hangs,
seeking a depth to descend to.

Something alien and unblinking
climbs through the mesquite in the yellow dawn,
sees you, alone on the white road,
and stares.

The bird killer

I am the stone spirited, the bird killer.
Life is distant from me, I am above it.
Death is on every screen, it does not
touch me.

A spring dusk on a lowland road.
The pheasant squats deep in the guts of the hedge, still,
watching, the white bar of his neck like a beacon in fog.
I aim.
One shot and the leaves erupt around him. A panic of wings.
Thin feather blades thresh the understorey. One shot.
Not enough.
I stumble in, parting tendrils with my fingers.
I reach down. He rolls and flails but is unable.
He is warm and moves in my hands
like a newborn. I do not have to. I have to.
I twist.

Still he moves. He does not stop for minutes.
Wings rise and fall like sails in the slightest breeze.
Life passes through my hands and disappears
in the darkening air above the fields,
away to the black trees.

I am rooted and empty.
I am the stone spirited, the bird killer.
Life is in my gift and is gone. I am hollow.
Now I shall feed.

stalker

death will cling to me like frost like the bracken
tick to the skin in high summer I will not smell it
but it will walk with me no love will dissolve it
they will go stonelike will spring back one of them is coming
one of the killers get beneath the rocks behind the thorns
get under the hedges be still do you smell it
one of them is coming he brings the shadow press your body
flat in the hollow press your ears to your back still your wings pray
that he passes

How it is done

Here you are, you sit between two worlds,
you are an animal.
The Earth is exposed to you as rock
beneath a spring.
You see more than you speak
because that it is how it is done.

But at night and in silence
you are alone on the barrow with the wind
on your brown skin, and in the dark
you hear the cries of old gods
and see the distant watchfires flicker.
You are a beast, a flat footed ape. You squat
by streams and hunt down that
which is greater than you.
You are clever and hungry and foul breathed.
You will kill because you must.
You are human. You see
more than you speak because that
is how it is done.

Angles

But what is this:
you have bought the universities?

We are coming for you.
We will push you down and hold you
under. We have long memories.

Now: we are in the universities.
Our thoughts fly and grow bold in the light.

Half a century: we marched to hold you off
we built a structure to contain you.

One century: you closed the mills and the mines.
You did not say sorry. They were yours,
you did not have to.

Two centuries: you took our land
for your sheep, for your ha has.
Into the cities we trailed, to the mills, the mines.

Three centuries: you took our boys in the night.
You packed them close by the gunwales
to destroy a foreign tyrant in the name of a foreign tyrant.

Four centuries: you rode in with your greaves, your breastplates.
You demanded again our billhooks
and our blood. You said your god was hungry.

Five centuries: we said
the hunger never changes, only the god.

Six centuries: every summer we loaded
a tenth of our labour into your barns.

Seven centuries: we thought we had found him, then.
We followed him but he was cut down
and we behind him.

Eight centuries: we watched you fight
amongst yourselves. As ever you offered us
nothing.

Nine centuries: you burned our farms and our children.
You ringed us with stone and rewrote our stories.

Ten centuries: the devil raged across the sea
and did not stop when he reached landfall.

Fourteen centuries: we were at peace
and free in our fields.

We are coming for you.
We will push you down and hold you
under. We have long memories.

Sixteen centuries: we burned their round houses
and took their fields for our own.

Master Race

It is often that I hate my Humanity.
A race of salesmen for whom a fury of execution
bequeaths the rights of a Maker. Beware:
We are coming, with veins of steel and souls radioactive
with self love, the pain of possibility sparking
in the pores of Our forelimbs. Do you see
what We have created? Do you understand
what We are? We are coming for you
to make you Useful.

You will love Us in time. You will
grow to. You must. There:
you have brushed against Our weak spot.
Tell us We matter.

Lost

Forcing myself down, into this role again,
I do not ask why or what for or if it matters –
certainly not that. There is no
time. There is a Judgement upon us
and we must busy ourselves denying its approach.

Behind the curtain we may speak to the priest as a stranger
provided we do not see his face.

I am not a religious man
because it has been disproved, as far as I have enquired,
but I bear a certain respect for the Believer.
The Believer may not long for the Judgement but perhaps
when it approaches the Believer is prepared.
I am not prepared. Nothing has been done.
I am fearful, when I am honest, and I am lost.
We are lost. We are all
lost, aren't we?

Behind the curtain we may speak to the priest as a stranger
provided we do not see his face.

I saw the Horned God

I saw the Horned God
of the Woods, in a stand
of poplar on the banks of the Thames
where it curls like a centipede
exposed to the sun through the fields
of Gloucestershire. It was early
morning. Politics, he said,
is killing you.

There was nothing human in him
yet there was something of me.
Why do you do it, he asked –
this willed reshaping of beyond?
Do you think the winds are in your hands?
Why must you look forward
when you should look around?
In the trees he seemed unborn,
grown from the silted soil, here,
always here, soul rough as bark,
feet planted.

We have dominion, I said.
We may not deserve it, but we have it:
what would you do?
Things will be done if I speak
or stay silent. They must be the right things.
We must fight!
In the leaves he moved
Incomprehensibly, so that life breathed
through them, impossible
to ignore, to explain.
He smiled. You have dominion? he replied –
he was almost kind –
I wish someone had told me.

Upland

It is cold and the stink of death is on the moor
and in the affliction of starlings,
in their wheeling. Some great turbine of wings
planted in the field's earth, turning
me with it, unwilling. A death has occurred
at a distance. It has been in my belly
all morning, it was not expected.
But nothing stops the birds or the wind
they navigate. I never count them.
They always come back.

Changeling

I have told you before, I have told you
so many times about this. You know
how much you anger me.

Do you know what a parent's love is?
You, who have always thought it was all
limitless. Oh, you have a child's mind.
The fields lie in shadow beyond your gaze
and when you close your eyes they disappear.

I give you what you ask for,
you ask for more. I leave you
alone in the place, you wreck it all.
You consume everything but the mess.
You cry when I fly at you, you plead,
you are always sure you will win out.

You will not always win out.

See, I have been thinking, back
to your birth and before. And I believe
you are a faerie child, spawned
on some distant star, left in my bed
for mischief. Mischief there has been, child,
but think on this: if you are not mine,
then I am not yours. Then it is open season,
child. Then there is a shift,
an alteration.

I know you now,
changeling.

Meetings

I would be happy as a minor poet.
The ballads of my ancestors come to me in dreams.
Duty to them a girdle or a burrowing root,
mine only to write them down.

Only to listen for the change in air pressure
that signifies the coming of images.
Here, now, is a bridle and heather,
water over limestone and the wind
that comes over the tops, determined.
Here, now, the sea
wrapping calmly around dark harbours
and a man and a woman on a headland
their fingers linked unseen beneath wool and cotton.

This cannot be, and it is.
This will link us until we die
and then it will link others.
The sea could take us now
but we would not be free of this.

Kidland

a Utopia of One

He came when the summer was high
to the dark false forests of the Kidland
where light does not go and people do not go
and trees are without branches because it suits us
that they should go naked.
Where the woods were on his map they were not on the land;
their boundaries fluid like floodwater they moved
across the peat at our command.
He came from the south, up the Border County Ride,
up Clennel Street where the homesick Roman
spat into the foul northern cloud.
At Wholehope, beside the track, he found a sheep byre
with strange, shuttered half windows.
For a night he bedded there, then rose
when the strained dawn woke him. The cloud
was low, the air hung with fine droplets.
He packed what he had and moved
north east, towards the black line half hidden in the white fog,
into the Kidland.

For three days he walked the tyred tracks
through the silent forest, observing what it held.
He followed the burns to their springheads
on the shoulders of the empty edges
and walked the banks of the Alwin, damp

and unannounced. He drank from each,

the water sharp with a dark iron,

and he surveyed every rise for its light.

For two hours he sat on the dark peak at Peat Law

in the uncorrupt needles, awaiting the sun.

When it never came he did the same at Dryhope,

then Nettlehope and Middle Hill.

Not finding what he wanted he inscribed a circle

around the Kidland and paced it, on the empty backs of the Cheviots,

from Wether Cairn to Bloodybush.

He walked it twice until he saw what he needed.

From the shoulder of Wether Cairn he followed a fence

which cut a line between the trees and the cottongrass

which took him past unnamed falls and through the nervous Alwin

which led him then up dark contours

to the clearing at Kidlandlee

where Roland stood, ankle deep in shit, his back

to the wall of trees, looking across the roof

of his hillturned barn, held together with rope and blistered

iron. The high cup of the clearing bowed its head

before the enfolding scarp of the woods,

on parade before their masters.

Beyond the dark Kidland he saw to the east the open lands

where the farming was good, and beyond them

the northern sea. Seventeen years,

he thought, and all I have is this view of the sea.

The sea: last redoubt of free creatures.

Soon we will find them and we will farm them too, if they prove
Useful, if we do not kill them first. Seventeen years
and tomorrow this place will lie quiet as if I were never here.
But there is nothing to be had this way,
the hills pay nothing now but silence.
I have been here and farmed it and now
I must go. No sound came from the now empty barn.
From the now empty fields rose a glory of finches,
spinning from the grasses, dipping diving scattering
gathering and wheeling off together
to the river.

Three contours down he watched the slight figure move
from the long dark barn to the small house and burn
into a rectangle of light. The afternoon
was slowing and something approached.
He climbed the stile that tied defiant fields
to the wood's weak light. The path led him down again
to the east. It narrowed, then it faded and left him
alone and unguided. On all sides the paper skin pines
stood unloved. Dead was the ground, dead
were the branches, green still were the hopeful crowns
calling up to the light.
There was little left when he came to the clearing
he had seen from the mountain. The small rise was grassed,
pinned by a circle of sky, a column of cooling air.
All around rose the purple trees.
He unshouldered his pack. This will be, he said,
where I build it.

The sun rose and the beasts and Sarah,
later. She bound her red hair then bound the blind
and watched the finches in the field below.
She made coffee, unfolded her map across the table.
To the east, she thought, through the trees
and upwards to the flat tops that ring them. Today
these tops will be my goal and whatever I pass on
the journey I shall learn from.
The day burned early so that even the Kidland looked
inviting. She cradled the cooling mug in both hands, knelt
on the white sill, watched the heather evolve as the sun took
　　then left it.
Beauty, she thought, is in the rough things. Like God
we set them going, then watch to see where they take themselves.
But God has more patience, more indifference by far.
We close in when we see rebellion to be crushed
through our will, misery to be relieved through our genius.
Too little trust and too much compassion: is this why God
is so disappointed in His children?
Across the field, past Roland's farm, she followed a track
which became a path, which became a myth
on a map until it reached a stile and beyond it a blackness
of depth and straight lines. The path led her down
through the sharpness, down a steep slope to the east.
It narrowed then faded until she was alone and unguided, until
she saw in the darkness a dim coming light:
sunlight, falling through a solitary gap, aiming
for a small green rise in which was some strange thing,

some den of canvas and plastic, of pots and blankets and ash,
a complexity of bare human comfort strung out
upon a spiderweb of rope and baling twine, and at its centre
a thin pale creature with a light in its eyes
which smiled at last when a smile was needed,
yet strangely as if there were something barren at its root.
He blocked the path, his spider den snagged on the bare, black
droplet ended twigs around the tiny clearing.
It was hard to pass without some word, impossible.
Hello, she said, it is a beautiful morning.
All mornings are beautiful he said, if you know
how to look at them, and most things are beautiful here
if you work to understand them. Where are you from?
What is your name? What are you doing here?
My name is Sarah, she said, I am staying in the house
at Kidlandlee. A holiday. A week.
She had no reason to tell him. She doubted herself
for telling him. And you? she replied, because she must.
You ... and this?

He said I left the cities of Babylon and I came
here, to the Wild, to where I thought I would find the Wild,
to a place where the darkness is a different colour.
There is lead in my blood, a numbness in all of my fingers:
this is what England has given me.
We are a leaden race, a numb people
nursing our yellow volumes while America's empire
smothers us with its dying breath. Here I am a man without a country.

The smell of this forest floor could be any in the hemisphere.
What I see of the sky is not written in any language.
Here are the Woodwose the Green Man the saucer eyed dogs
of the eastern fells. At night the Wild Hunt passes
above the pines aflame, howling for the blood of Men
but it shall not have mine. He smiled, a distance in it.
I am free here, he said, free
from groups and guidelines and the thinking of people
who do not think except to follow the others.
Here I am free because I am exposed,
here I shall build a Utopia of One.
He smiled again, this time recognisable to her
this time come back to her world. It is easier this way, he said.
No bending with the will of people
no absorption into the mass
no dilution of the image. And – now he grinned –
no meetings. For that alone
who would not flee to the hills?
She smiled too then, nervously. He was interesting and not
to be trusted and possibly to be feared.
What was he doing here in this place,
in the darkness and depth of this place?
Have you lived, he asked, in the cities of the south?
I live there now, she said. And are they killing you?
he asked; of course they are. It is good, she replied, to escape
sometimes. But I like the people. Nobody
wants to be lonely. I do, he said, and he said it fiercely.
It is only through loneliness that you meet the world

on equal terms, on anything like equal terms.
What do you say to all those people? Can you remember
the last thing you said that was of consequence,
the last thing you heard?
There is nothing of consequence in the cities of the south.
Nobody listens there, nobody hears.
One impulse from this forest betters a year of it,
you will get nothing from those people but disappointment.
I am certain of that if I am certain of anything.
Sarah did not think a reply was wanted, did not think
he was the kind who would have heard it.
You should stay here, he said, the spider light in his eyes.
This is where life is. Real life, I mean. Perhaps
you would be surprised. You may even be converted.
Converted? she thought. Who is this missionary of the Man formed
Wild and where, what is his god? Or is he his own?
She was polite in replying, she allowed herself even
a small, crooked smile which acted upon him
though she did not know it. Not for me
she said. What would I tell people? I am not that type.
My sense of duty is too strong.
He smiled once more, her words ran by him without catching.
I must get on, she said. I aim for the tops. I may
see you again. You will he said,
you will.

Dusk settling down on the land that does not shift,
that has not shifted for millennia beneath footfall of men and horses

beneath tyres and the low pressing sky, that did not shift
now as he trod the path up the hill through the woods
to the house. The black
broke into ascending blue as the forest gave way
to the unploughed meadow below the farm. He took
the stile in one awkward stride, his boots touched down
at the low watermark of a bog which kept the field in winter
and there, beside his boot, by the fence
of wood and wire, something moved. Feeble and determined
to escape, believing all could be well again,
that all that was needed was will, a crow,
slow and heavy, lay on its side in the cottongrass.
He knelt and gently lifted it from its prison, Earth.
Weakly it half stretched its wings, splayed its yellow toes
softly scratched him. He brought it to his face
turned it slowly, examined it. He saw
no wound. What is wrong, little one? he asked,
what has grounded you? He cradled it gently
its feathers the dark beauty of an oil slick
its warmth, like his, entirely animal.
Night is coming crow, he said, and what will you do?
A bird without wings does not survive the coming of the dark.
Do you know it is all over or do you still believe?
Can you picture the end? Does your fear have a shape
or do you still expect a miracle? You are beautiful,
it is a shame. You have put me
in a position. What do I do now – leave you
or end it swiftly? Perhaps I should,

but I will not. I believe in miracles too.
How else would I stay alive?
For a long time he looked into the bird's black eye,
wondered what it saw. Its eyelid, grey, translucent
beat against the jeweled jet iris like the heart
of the world. Its beak, scratched and soiled, opened
and closed slowly, slightly, as if it sought for words:
Man, you are grounded also, let us exchange
pity. Greatly you have sinned against us. Still
I am grateful for the warmth of these hands.
He smiled at himself, placed the bird gently
on the ground again. Crows do not speak, he said,
except in poems.

You, she said, an accusation.
He turned and she was there, just yards away.
I came looking for the first star of evening, she said. The pink sky is
beautiful. At night here there are no lights, it is so easy
to adjust to. In the cities, he said, you must numb yourself to live.
Here all you need do is breathe out.
You are strange, she said: a thought
which became words by mistake.
But he did not mind; he smiled.
May I offer you a drink? he asked
bowing slightly, I have a good malt
and you feel the night intensely in the trees.
She said yes before she thought,
then surrendered to the coming. Lead on

she said.

Three mugs of malt and the darkness was speaking,
and him. There was nothing he could say but
of who he was, of himself of his project of the greatness
he saw in everything but people. She had tried
but his eyes burned for nothing else and now
she was listening, because listening was all he would allow.
Where is the urgency? he was saying. Can you not see
how things are? The great forests are burning, the great forests
of the world. The breath of your lungs is taken from you
and what do you do? There are a million jewelled creatures
that you will never see, that the world
will never see again. There is poison in the water
and in the air and in every cell that you are made of.
Poison: our gift to the world. Do you ever wonder
What the place would be like without us? Free
I would say, to breathe again.
Holding her chipped mug, the night still warm, she said
I don't see you saving what you hymn from your canvas. I see you
drinking in a dark forest far from anywhere. Talk
is cheap. He did not scowl, his face was open.
I have withdrawn, he said, I will play
no part, I will not be corrupted. Perhaps it is pure souls
not hope that will save us. Perhaps, she said, there is no saving us.
Why do you talk like a priest? Does it give you your purpose?
Your pure soul may please you;
the birds in the trees please me, and my humanity,

complicated and compromised and often sinning.
I am afraid of those who seek purity, I am afraid
of what their seeking will release.
You do not understand, he said,
drinking. Why would you? You have not seen it.
You have not made the promise. It is easy for you to dismiss me
and vital. If I am right, where does that leave you?
You would have to act, to change your world.
What would you tell people? What about your comforts, your small
distractions from the Great Beauty? No, far better to mock us,
those of us who can no longer stand it, who will not
stand for it. Laugh: you are free to. You will see.
Or if you never see, at least for a moment I did
and then I knew what everything was for and what I am here
to do.
There was silence after this. He drew breath, she smelt
the whisky on it and wondered then if she should be here.
She made to stand. He stood with her. Going? he asked.
Don't go, have I angered you? Angered, no,
she thought; frightened, yes. But she said
no, I am tired, I should leave, it is late and I need
my small distractions. He flinched and moved at her, he drew
close, she could smell again the spirit. I do not mean,
he said, to insult you, but you must know
the beauty that is here. You must know what you stand to lose.
I think you have it within you. I see it in your eyes, I
sense it. The Wild is in you. Bring it out.
She stepped away, the firelight receding. Did you say, she asked,

you had a torch? She could hear her own voice, the fear.

He heard nothing. He moved faster he touched her he bent

his head towards hers, she flinched she stepped

back, bent her ankle on a stump, righted herself.

Please, she said, but he was not listening. She realised now

the mistake she had made. Bring it out he said

bring out the Wild. Get off, she said. And again: get off, no.

She fought, but weakly and he had her too close

and he was not here, he was not here at all.

He forced her back into the corrugated bark of a young pine

which moved as he tore from her what he could and needed

to, then took her to the sharp citrus of the forest floor

where she gave in. They were too far from anyone and in his eyes

was something she had seen before, once and long ago, and knew

was not to be fought.

Afterwards she lay cold and half stripped, sore

and wet and open but she did not shiver. He did

and she watched him avoid her gaze, crouched half stripped too

on his knees, breathing hard and not moving his eyes.

Small and violated he knelt. You are in my power now

she thought, and as usual I am too late.

Is this, she said, your Utopia?

Oh I am proud to have been a part of it.

It was not the cities, was it, that made you a destroyer?

She sat up and began to pull herself into some kind of order.

He did not move, she did not look at him again, she did not

have to. In the almost silent blackness she stumbled

away, aching groping at the cold trunks, heading she hoped

for Kidlandlee. For a long time she could sense him, low and unmoving
not contrite but sunken, knowing again it was in him
and knowing what and not wanting to, and all of this she felt
as if it were her kneeling cold and white, angry and disgusted and thrilled
on the stinking sponge of the dead forest floor.

When he rose himself, the Kidland was still. He did so slowly
as if to live now were a lesson in the casual pain of his Natural justice.
Why did I do it? he asked himself aloud, and knew as he did so
that he asked for show, though there was no-one to hear
or care. You did it because you wanted to, because you could,
because you are an animal, because you will escape. You did it
because this is what men do when the walls are lowered and the ropes
removed. Applaud yourself: you have shown an honesty tonight
that few men show. You came here to seek the animal,
now you have found the animal.
Now you are the wild god of the world,
now you have given the pain you must give to be free.
Be indifferent now, be king of this place, anointed
with the oils of the old ceremony.
He stood, shrugging his clothes on.
Stars, he said, I need
stars.

Roland shuttered the door and flicked off the light.
All around was the darkness of an inhuman midnight.
He walked slowly across the yard, which was piled and scattered
with what he had built and had now pulled down.
Footless cauldrons holed buckets rusted sickles a wooden barrow
stacked with sheared scythe handles. Over the valley,
across the plains, there was nothing burning. Not one light
save the sometimes swift headlights that rose over a brow then dipped
beyond. He craned his neck.
The Milky Way spread itself above him. What is this?
he asked again. How many of these stars are already dead?
If the universe is expanding what is it expanding
into? Where is my imagination? Tied to the dirt
when it should have been soaring. And at once
he wanted to drive one last time down the track
from the house to the Alwin. Again
he wanted to roll, no lights no engine windows down
through the black forest, see the stars above him
feel the damp air, hear the owls, be as close to the night
as the age would allow. He took his keys
and opened the gate.

From the wall of trees he stepped
out onto the white silence of the track,
looking up, not back, looking up when he needed finally
to look around him. Roland felt a shattering of his expectations
something solid passing across the edge of his vision
the rough, tearing jerk of a world changing.

He brought his senses back to the road, stopped fast
opened the door, saw him where he had known he would be.
At the edge of the track, dark in the ditch, fast
against a dying trunk, dying he half sat.
Surprised, knocked out by it all
weeping blood from his opened belly
choking on air like a landed fish,
fallen through the drumskin to the void beneath.
He gasped. He would not look down. He looked up.
If there is a god, he said, he is a poet with a sense
of humour. Or else he is a banker with none.
Or neither. Ignore me, I did not expect this, I prepared
nothing. Again he gasped and his face
contorted with disappointment.
There was nothing more. The stars
rewarded Roland with what he had sought
but now he was unseeing.

A year on, dead stems in plastic
mark the tree. Sarah and her sense
of duty, of pity, of some dark element
she would never now be rid of, and the need
to close the wild circle.
Nothing else, and she
is long gone south.

and the trees

and the trees on the hill stand waiting to reclaim the field
and the field lies yellow and cut beneath the sky
and the sky hangs grey above the grassline
and the grasses quieten at the approach of night
and night comes and I rise and move towards the trees
I hope they will have their way soon
and I tell them so

The god of the birds

A magpie there was in a sparrow's nest,
caught feasting on rich yolks by the god of the birds,
who had been watching him for some time.
The magpie looked up to see his god
bear down on him from a golden sky. Paralysed,
he cowered. I have warned you! cried the god of the birds.
More than once I have punished you, destroyer
of the sons of your fellows. Now my patience is ended.
What will you do? cried the magpie, half-defiant,
half afraid. I will banish you, replied his god. I will make you
a Man.

Your wings will lose their feathers.
You will learn to grasp. I will encase you in cloth,
give you a Man's limbs, a Man's head
to furnish you with a sky's-worth of words for war,
a nestful of excuses for devouring
your young. You may keep your cunning
which you refuse to call deceit; share it with others
who, like the birds, cannot look ahead but only
to the side; who, like the birds, rise above all else that is living.
You will be at home there. Among Men, your talents will bear flower
and, like all flowers touched by them, will wither and die.

Seeing his fate, impotent and angered, the magpie cried out.
You made me this way! he spat. I eat the world
because you made me to eat the world. Now you punish me
for what you have done. The god of the birds
smiled, alighted silently on the branch beside him.
You are not the first to complain, he said.
I am also the god of Men. Often they rail at me,
sometimes they strike out on their own, thinking
to build themselves a world with their heads only.
But they can never escape what I have put inside of them.
Come, now: there is much to be done. You must
be hungry.

The pool

At the Dawn of Time
was a pool around which two Men sat.
Early Men, though they did not know this.
Clear was the water in the pool.
Clear were their minds, for
they knew no different.
They had no speech, only the use
of their hands and their bodies.
It seemed to one that
the motion of the fever trees in the wind,
when reflected in the water,
gave life to its surface.
It seemed to him that the water was alive.
He could not say so.
He had no vision of saying so.
Instead he looked into the eyes of the second Man
who, squatting, returned his gaze.
It seemed to both that they were thinking the same thing
which, being thought, became true.
The water lived,
like the Men and the fever trees
and the things that moved in the fever trees
and beneath them, and at night
above them.
Everything lived.
How could it not be so?
There were no thoughts which said it could not be so.

i

i cannot speak to the whale
and the porpoise will not listen
i have mined and quarried the seas
but there are cultures in the depths that do not need me

and i think it hurts that even if i find them
i will still be me
still the seeker and the ravager
lover of mystery and destroyer of mystery

wanderer self-excised from the Earth
there is nothing i can say now
they will hear

Emperor

I have seen
what no one should. My snowplough skin
has razored polished darkness.

I have seen,
with others' eyes, chaotic kingdoms
fall to dirt white armies.

I have flown
through tears of smoke, through waterfalls
of forest dust and home.

I have swept
the salt away, the clouds before me,
scoured the screaming Earth.

I have drunk
what no one could, who lacks my throat,
have tasted growth to death.

But I can feel
no searing pain, no slow dissolving
platitudes, for I

I have hid my heart in a butterfly.
I cannot be killed and I
I can never cry.

A chaos of you

The trees are a chaos of you.
They climb from the soil clean
in their unpaintable colours.
Every lilac blossom an idea
every snakebone branch a desire
every breeze that moves them an unhad adventure.
They dream, rooted, of the hills beyond their kerbside
and in the autumn, unexpected but meant for the moment,
their dreams are carried away to be born.

Black Beck

Down in the valley there is damage.
A series of small devastations has loaded
the years onto the land like rocks
upon the chest of a sinner.
Rubber steel asphalt aluminium:
there is to be no rest.

Here there are changes too,
but I am not qualified to read them.
All I see is an eternity of water.
Below the fells, huddled like brothers
with closed shoulders of stone,
the Black Beck runs across the rocks
through the moss and the peat
winds through ten acres of bog and settles into the tarn.
I have seen ravens and little else.
I am just passing through and see little else.

I may have a son and he a daughter.
In a century she may walk here.
The ravens will be dead, the valley overcome
but the Black Beck will run on.
Water has seen more than it speaks.
It has seen the kist builders
pass and the miners. It has flowed
over the bodies of the ravens.
I am just passing through.

Fly Agaric

We push the Earth's blood up
through its skin. We make you
an offering.

We are legion around
the birch roots: when the days
grow short we rise

beneath you and beyond you.
Your naming holds no truth
here. We divide

and die and live again
small and unambitious.
Pay attention

to our lesson.

I do not want to hear about your baby

I do not want to hear about your baby. I swear
if I hear about your baby one more time
I will burn this city to cinders.
I am glad that you are happy and hidden
from any thing that may move you
outside yourself. I am
overjoyed at your expression of milk.
Just do not speak to me ever again of any of it.
Inside me is some creature that would
tear your small happiness apart
were I to take my warning hand from its collar.
It has not fed for years. It has been hell for me
to break it. I would need to let go
for just a second.

This morning I walked in a forest of lime before the city awoke.
Spring came early and wood anemones
exhaled for the light. The wide leaves were
green as you have never seen them
and there was the smell of death.
Sweet it was and painful and thrilling: a fox
I guessed in a dungeon of leaves.
It will be gone in a week
and life was the greener for it.
I thought of you then, and your baby
and your expression of milk and your smiling, quiet
desperation, and I was young.

There are no ghosts

Above the valley, below the crags but clear
of the treeline, is an old hunting lodge.
A hall once, then an inn, now a ruin: stones
and ivy and thin trees scratching a living
in the old fireplace.

I come here searching for ghosts,
but I find nothing.
No smuggler left a lasting mark. No
wheel ruts, no taste on the wind.
When I walk the track to the ruin I find
nothing. I see nothing but cowshit
and boulders. The dead
have nothing to say to me.

As gifts I bring them false memories
and some kind of ancient longing
I can never quite come at and never
shake off. But it is no good.
No-one is coming back. No-one
is listening. There are no ghosts
and our sins are our own.

The getting free

She is wondering what colour to paint the nursery wall and she is
decaying. It may be that there are other universes
in which she is not yet born or has other choices.
Still, she is fighting time with the certainty
of defeat.

A reason, then, for joy,
for defeat will come to victory in the end.
What bridges you passed under will never be known nor
matter. You have this, my love: make it all
then burn away knowing you were here and you defied them.
And hold on to me as you shake them off.
Be strong enough to turn away from their ideas,
their schemes for betterment, their necessary proposals,
their desperate carving of their names in the sandstone of time.
Be strong enough to come with me and keep me
strong as we build our house by the lake in the mountains.
Death scorns ideas and so does
life: a getting free and then
the final getting free.

Parable of the tares

The band returns to the city in the hollow
and the crowd goes wild. Music arrows up above the mass
like the thin birch to the light. In cities
all across this hollow world there is light, there is
music. Sing, people, sing; your cities are legion
and your time is short. Band, play them out.

I am the blood and the body
I am the resurrection and the life

You have made wonders, they are wide and tall wonders. The white fox
envies your warmth, the dun buzzard your safety, the grey whale
your certainty. Nothing else has matched you, not from want
but through fortune. Sing, world, of what is fading.

None comes unto the Kingdom but through me

Nothing is permanent, everything pulling apart, cascading
away from the highest peaks. Vibrate the strings of this once green world
one final time, make merry, go with laughter
and with fury, almost-masters.

There being tares amongst my wheat
I gather it into my barn

Something in the air

The huntsmen are riding in the West.
Through the winter woods their hounds are calling
as mist rises in bands between the birches.

There is a heavy, heartless beauty anchored
in the black soils of Europe,
silent and uncaring, overlooked
by its busy patrons, waiting
as the Earth turns towards the dark.
We have learned much about ourselves
and little about each other and now
there is something in the air.
Search for it in the soft fire of an autumn dawn –
you will see nothing, yet your future
is held in trust by the seas.

At the edge of the woods a black shape
bursts from the trees and panics
across the frost white field.

About the Author

Photo: Jyoti Kingsnorth

PAUL KINGSNORTH has worked in an orangutan rehabilitation centre in Borneo, as a peace observer in the rebel Zapatista villages of Mexico and as an assistant lock-keeper on the river Thames. He has also worked as a journalist on the comment desk of the *Independent*, as commissioning editor for *openDemocracy* and as deputy editor of *The Ecologist* magazine.

He is the author of two non-fiction books: *One No, Many Yeses* (Simon and Schuster, 2003), an investigative journey through the 'anti-globalisation' movement, and *Real England* (Portobello, 2008) an exploration of the disappearing cultures and landscapes of his home country.

His poetry has been published in magazines including *Envoi, Agenda, Iota, Reach, The Lighthouse, Staple* and *nthposition*. He won the Poetry Life National Competition in 1998, and was named BBC Wildlife Poet of the Year in the same year. Kidland is his first collection.

In 2009, he co-founded the Dark Mountain Project, a literary and cultural movement for an age of ecological collapse and social upheaval.

His website is www.paulkingsnorth.net